The Big Wheel

Andrew Nightingale

Oversteps Books

First published in 2009 by   Oversteps Books Ltd
                                  6 Halwell House
                                  South Pool
                                  Nr Kingsbridge
                                  Devon
                                  TQ7 2RX
                                  UK

www.overstepsbooks.com

Oversteps Books acknowledges with thanks the financial assistance
of Arts Council England, South West

Printed in Great Britain by imprint digital, Devon

Acknowledgements

Individual poems have previously appeared in Alba (online), Anon, The Argotist (online), Aught (online), Diagram (online), Dream Catcher, Envoi, Intercapillary Space (online), Iota, The Journal, Magma, Manifold, Moria (online), Nth position (online), Orbis, Parameter, The Physik Garden (online), Poetry Salzburg Review, Poetrybay (online), Poly Magazine (Falmouth), Pulsar, South, Staple, Stride Magazine (online), Tears in the Fence, Tremblestone, The Ugly Tree, Voice and Verse, and Wandering Dog (online).

Contents

We turned back

We pitched our tents on the fringe of the desert.
We posed for a group photograph.
But somehow we knew we were already too late.
We had travelled for days from Persia,
Mongolia, Turkestan.
We had jewellery, spices,
ritual incense.
But somehow we knew it was all too late.
Does land sink or the ocean rise?
Does day follow night or night follow day?
One thing was sure, our goddess was dead.
We played cards until morning
then methodically loaded the camels.
We had to see the ruined temple,
touch the seven shredded veils.
But we knew for sure our goddess had died.
We travelled on, arguing
about pointless matters of protocol,
until we came to an inn.
We left our gifts with the poor
and turned back.

Exquisite mostly

a postcard
posted three weeks ago
with just one word "Ricordi!"

in the institute
there is a disease
that kills romantics

flowers and cigarettes
long literary letters
and a shoal of little stories

she looked very ill
in intolerable foreign hotels
wearing short skirts

charm has bold equipment
absurdity, zest
and the briefest stories

dilated eyes
a bird of paradise
hateful now and numb

a private tower with an open fire
makes a pleasant room
for observation

clearly dying
under observation
peeling potatoes then

stop

then more peeling potatoes
and smoking
above the cowshed

it would be fun
on a boat like a leaf
rowing into a perfect moment

a muff, a fur, a hat
and do not quite forget
well-founded gossip

letters, flowers and cigarettes
homely ministrations
lying awake conscious

everything is material
a satirist is conscious of everything
childhood, adulthood, everything

everything is about stories
as though telling stories
or smoking and listening

a hat on a nail
cuckoos, silken grass
and shadows racing

harmony developed
drawn and moved, suffering animal
in a fur, scraping carrots

in a fur

malice in seaside houses
railway stations and park benches
short skirts and no not a single word

in a spring of bluebells
written up badly, superficial
smart, fashionable, cheap

do not quite forget
the addiction and the treatments
the death of Moses

rich material, deep and sharp
an animal
who suffers clearly

dying
in a pleasant room
with no matches, no paper

nothing for a fire
coughing blood
in wooded country half-understood

under observation
gossip and malice
pursued by sharks

and
Ricordi!
perfect moments...

Magic theatre

Whenever I fall asleep
curtains hitch themselves apart
on a tiny wooden puppet theatre.
Hidden candles bring up a flat painted Prague
and snatches of a single violin drift,
testing fragments of a Slovak dance.

Then the usual puppets clamber on
and work through the same old repertoire,
the same chunks of dialogue,
off-hand as if for an umpteenth rehearsal.
It appears to be a broken magnum opus, mostly lost,
the few remaining scenes banal out of context.

If I could just replay this while I was awake,
or if some Mephisto was available to translate,
then perhaps the puppetry would stop.
But they are like evangelists speaking in tongues:
the only word I recognise is Romany for tomorrow.
And the same word also means yesterday.

The deer healer

The painstakingly restructured heartland
of the business liaison park
boasts grazing deer, a lake
and acres of mature woodland.

A relaxed executive directorate
is returning from the hunt
and entering the clubhouse.

On a bed of lettuce leaves,
the magical strength of muscle,
in its nebula of gristle and bone,
is teased apart by indolent knives.

"Let me put it to you simply," he smiles
unassumingly, "who pays your wages?"

With the dumb stare of a blank cheque
I walk in a dungeon of woods with his words
following a step behind me.

Skills of the fool: don't ask,
keep to your corner, and to what you know,
the healing of deer, how to tend the herd,
the nurture of health and strength.

Lynmouth

Lynmouth, Watersmeet,
the time the water pump
packed up in a cloud of steam.
We left the car and walked
down towards the gorge.
The rivers were in flood.
We were both so angry.

Watching two rivers meet,
we caught the rush, were silent,
kissed, didn't want to talk.
This water worked:
the car was all words
water wanted to resist,
like *tension* and *torque*.

The RAC man came and went,
came back and began
to remanufacture flow.
We stood in that valley soaked
in white noise, in drenching mist,
trying to understand.

Resurrection sonnets

1.

An obscure alley / in the heart
of blaring Naples. / My mother found
the church finally. / She'd dragged us
miles for this / in baking heat:
in two adjacent / glass display cases
husband and lover / stood long dead
and gone but / for blood vessels
clotted solid, preserved / forever. No-one has
recreated the poison / his wife concocted
to wreak this / revenge, stopped blood,
her poetic answer / to incontinent passions.
The vessels hinted / wireframe human outlines
from fingertips to / penis, immaculate, fleshless.
This way immortality / can be achieved.

2.

Her father taught / speaking in tongues,
hit her because / a household needs
authority and control. / She had to
speak the Word / in Pentecostal meetings
but when hit / she said nothing,
she wouldn't surrender / a single sound.
Mute like a / beast under dominion
but escaping, born / again into veganism,
not scriptural, not / her steak stuffed
father's loveless duties. / You can think
like an animal. / And I came,
her stray lurcher, / to protect her
from her father's / laws and inanimate
thought and I'll / try killing him.

3.

Fat on lard   cake, the baking
that his mother   always keeps flowing,
stretch marks where   his belly overawes
lazy trousers, nevertheless   his mind is
monkish on metaphysics   and illuminated manuscripts.
Mother thinks appetite   will help him
off this obsession   they call schizophrenia.
Feed him back   into her conspiracy.
Neuroleptics, dripping and   his rosary beads,
empty signs left   where he was.
It spirals beyond   measure, dizzy hermeneutics
and therapy take   their toll on
enlightenment. Fatten him   like a pig
for a celebration   of motherly slaughter.

4.

It's well known   that Albertus Magnus,
theologian and sorcerer,   spent thirty years
creating a curious   speaking iron man
that answered questions   infallibly. Planets dictated
the unknown elements   in its construction.
Aquinas destroyed it   out of jealousy
I think. But   did you know
also that Magnus   had a pet
snake he was   awfully fond of?
And that this   android ate it,
every last shred   of its skin?
The android required   a constant diet
of snake meat   and when archaeologists
found it recently   it was pot-bellied.

5.

Mountains, lake, lemons:	Torbole, here Goethe
fell in love.	Through honeymoon dripped
satellite channels, news	of the Temple
Solaire's massacre in	the ice-cream Alps.
Goethe the romantic	under olive trees
drinking wine with	a new Margareta
(not the pizza)	would be bored
by their eternity.	It comes from
long roasted winters	of Rosicrucian mysticism.
Basil's an anti-depressant:	in an Italy
still at home	with pagan masques,
and British poets	eternity seems unnecessary.
We liked Verona	but flew back
after a week	to forensic details.

6.

In this hell	I can't have
you. I can't	have you. You
are the quintessence	of all loves
I can't have.	There's nothing else
I want. Wanting	is the process
of consuming you.	This is hell
ruled by you.	The process of
becoming you from	the inside out,
of you reciprocally	eating me from
the core until	all that's left
is my ghost,	pale and plainly
in this hell	still where I
can't have you.	There's nothing else
to say. Wanting	you I want.

The groom remembers his dead mother

The best man remains standing.
About him heads droop, interrogate
an untouched soldier of cake.
The bride takes the groom's hand,
cups it in her cool palm.
Everyone prays.

I'm captivated by a glass, I gawp dumbly
at its transparent pod of Moët,
a glowing kernel of harvest moon,
and the constant stream of bubbles
like Saturday traffic on the motorway.
In the accelerating silence
I begin to imagine
I'm hearing the bubbles break the surface
each with a pin drop tinkle,
a steady prickle of sound,
the background hum of the universe
holding itself just above zero Kelvin.
Zoom in and the prickle magnified
is a solid wedge of white noise,
a snowstorm on television.

Then the best man speaks
(a minute has passed).
Guests shift, finger the stem of a glass,
uneasy for a joke,
and no-one notices bubbles any more.

The woodcarver

An old man is sitting by the Rialto.
He whittles at a figurine,
intricate fingers searching
for the human form
in the gnarl and knot of the seasons.

Each figurine becomes a languid adolescent,
a stretched uncluttered chord
placed once and left to sound
on a grand piano.

He died on a February night,
his stiff body propped on frosty cobbles.
They handled him like antique wood,
manoeuvring him onto a barge.

Then I found one floating. Quizzical,
she unnerves me with her doll's squint.
Washed of river slime, the little idol
is placed on my window sill.

Sometimes, on a windless dusk in Autumn
when I open the casement,
she sings softly in Latin,
the pale notes moving like candlelight
out over the Laguna Morta to the dead.

Powerless

The wind was aching in the pylons.

Soaked in sudden darkness,
as if the room had been a slide projected,
we fell into an ancient grotto.

We lit it with a candle each,
faces in haloes like painted saints,
eyes wet black and animal.

The wind was our secret ally,
agent provocateur. In collusion
we boiled water on the open fire,
instantly taken back a thousand years.

Electricity is a surface and beneath the surface
the nights are falling apart.
The national grid disturbs our dreams.

Always well-lit under strip lights
and confident of taking charge,
we were so used to just flicking a switch.
We needed time to readjust our actions,
our desires. We needed longer.
But the power came back on.

Fair meditations

Big Wheel

The view is beautiful from high above the fairground lights. The shrieks and cries, below among the rides, seem almost philosophical. I can't imagine wanting to get off. But the circle draws down and in.

Carousel

These are sinister journeys, chasing down some atrocity of gilt and lights and organ music that once took place in the nursery. It was before the millstone cracked the husk. Before the top came off the medicine.

Tunnel of Love

How can I separate the tunnel from the love that sits beside me? We travel together. The tunnel is nothing without us. We leave arm in arm, scoring points off each other. The tunnel keeps our kiss.

Hall of Mirrors

I see myself multiplied and disfigured, my own private army barring my exit. I must have wanted this ritual entrapment, to be lost but contained in grim replication, because I don't want escape to be too easy.

Dodgems

A car crash can be an infinitesimal pause, a brief moment of diamond-like reflection that gradually fills with pain. So it's rehearsed for the sake of all those little deaths that end in laughter.

Ghost Train

In luminous green, skeletons lurch and clatter. Training has made them jesters, cavorting and carousing in the dark. Elsewhere I believe, in another fair, there is an exquisite display of glow-worms accompanied by a lone bamboo flute.

Candyfloss

Sentiment spins sticky clouds, congealed and dangerous, a fibrous nausea. It now becomes possible to assess what kind of transformation I have wrought. Sweetened bile marks the pavement like a residue.

Big Wheel

The guard bar drops and locks shut. The carriage swings. We leave in small steps, rising by degrees but never out of sight, to a void enshrined by the lights below.

Paddington snowstorm

Under the clock in Paddington station.
His wrist flicks from jacket sleeve,
the practised art of a million glances:
the watch looks back.

In it a miniature scene
crowded with clockwork figures
hard to make out in a snowstorm.
He breathes on the face and wipes it,
peers into the glass,
furrowing his brow.

Fascinating. He can make out a room of little people,
all moving with a purpose but none quite real.
He can make out a clock and under it a man
who seems to suddenly flick his wrist and...

He hastily drops his arm.
Forgets to buy flowers.
The microcosm is still strapped on,
like a bomb beneath his cuffs,
when his date arrives.
Too late:
he looks at her and knows
she is only clockwork
like the miniature his watch controls.

A winter once before

The first flakes   precipitate
   by the force
    of my wish for it to snow:
       the clenched sky
is iron, tinged yellow.   It holds
   a sly and brittle wind,
a mesh of imminent ice
       poised waiting
while I wish for its incarnation.
   Six years ago
on Valentine's day it snowed.
Newly married   we had a white world
    looking in
   past the icing fresh
against the edge of the window.
Six years' hard work
    without snow and winter
has become   a faint whisper,
   weather warnings,
   a few words lifted in hope
from the road's   black ice.
  But tonight
    I can almost hear
     flakes
   starting to form.

Five short parables

1. The dripping tap

When his heart was beating fast
there were chasms between each drip.
When his heart was beating slowly
the drips seemed to race.

When he died...
he still hadn't had the leak fixed.

2. Stolen time

The time you steal from your duties
is made of silk, billowing under golden bracelets
that the sun sprinkles between leafy boughs.
Even doing nothing is a luxury and not a waste
and the disregard you show for your duties
is like the laughter of a friend.

3. Where the thinking goes

Wondering where her thoughts had gone
after she thought them, she searched
and found them with some biscuit crumbs, a pen
and some coins down the side of the sofa.

"So this is where they go," she thought,
but within an instant the thought had already slipped
out of reach into the arms of its ancestors
and she was staring blankly at the television.

4. A rug pulled away

When the rug was pulled away he found
antique wooden floorboards that, sanded down,
would be very chic.

When he pulled up the floorboards he found
a cellar that would be excellent for fine wines.

When he dug into the earth he found
a spacious grave dug lovingly by hand
from local soil.

5. Opening an account

I decided to leave my mark on the world
by opening an account. The indelible ripple
it sent through the physics
of our nation's assets will be a record
more final than pen applied
to a page without capital.

The end of the day

In this slow booming heat, the moon
floats like an impossible ice cube.
As the dregs of the sun glance sideways,
the moon is buoyed in a floodlit pool.
Why should I tell you this? For the pleasure
of recognition? There's nothing new here.
Some arbitrary Roman stood the same heat
and saw the same impossible moon
and thought of the pleasure of ice.

The moon is melting.
Today its ice is even more impossible than before.
I recline among Romans
who pick their teeth and wait for entertainment.
The mind that thinks of ice
sees a blade of grass and thinks of war,
sees the sun set and thinks of blood,
sees an empire die and raises a glass
to the new empire.

When I next drop ice
into Bombay Sapphire, I don't
think of the moon. I think of the associations
I make every day as if they're new, as if
they're not echoes of old atrocities.
Then I wash them through with juniper.

Trapdoor to China

The spade punctures turf, slips
through wet earth,
marks a circle, lifts
a slice of cake.
This first wedge repeated,
the foundations
opened on a Cornish lawn
for a mosaic bed,
a Taoist shrine to-be
freed from alien soil
as if by archaeology.

Tongue-like, a worm
hides methodically
in chocolate sponge.
My fingers are too clean,
weak in communion
with the native spade,
carrying foreign magnetism:
soap, PC, microwave.
I hover,
living like oil on water,
sleeping badly,
eating badly,
inventing dreams of China.

Valle Scura

The question is
          What is a pass?
There must be a place where transition lives
A valley where the pass is posed
And verbed into an answer

When you pass through Valle Scura
Don't think of passing for its own sake
It does no good
The valley is dark
             Vinegar to a summer fruit
Velvet isolation
          Curtained off by hissing rain
A vaporous chapel of rest
             Oh it urges rest
                  But don't rest
                      Pass
               Through the valley
       Bloodied by rosehips
Bruised by mushrooms
Veiled in the prophecies of the evergreen oak
Pass through the valley
The chapel of rest isn't for you
Vanity keeps you alive

The valley recedes
The path wakes from its daze
Vestiges of the question come back
What was it?
A conversation took place virtually unnoticed
You said (remember?)
          What is a pass?
             And the valley
                 Yes
          The valley answered
In the cleft heart of Valle Scura you heard
What the valley thought of passing

Marginal notes

Notes pencilled in the margins of Lavengro:
see favorite passage page 181
and Seven Pillars of Wisdom: that
asymptote is a line that approaches
but never meets a given curve.
His child, a one-year-old, escaped the blast.
She was an omission from the text.
September 1929, Exmouth 1940:
he was killed by a bomb with his wife.
And do you think that is the end of man?
Their child escaped the pull of the curve.
If I thought I heard him in a wind on the heath,
if I thought he was trying to tell me something,
that would be a kind of possession.
It depends on the locus of consciousness.
I was twenty-four when I heard.
He died then, off-duty.
There's an end of him brother, more's the pity.
What's mine is sometimes his.
On leave visiting a shoe shop in Exmouth,
he was a marginal incident, a bomb off target.
It's as if I changed my name. *Why do you say so?*
That would be reincarnation,
that I could live like a wind on the heath.
It depends on the locus of consciousness.
And the area under the curve.
It's *the same as talking like a fool.*
My mother keeps his books.
In sickness in blindness
I want to master his words.

Sibylline monologues
"The Dead came back from Jerusalem, where they found not what they sought" C.G.Jung, *Septem Sermones ad Mortuos* (1916)

Whose voice is whispering in the mountains?

A voice has woken where the woods are thick.
    It's climbing down towards the village.
        It's trying to move my pen
           and it's calling to the dead.

Whose voice dictates on the tongues of pines
    and pushes with the white water
        down through narrow gorges?

The pines collude in rites of wood smoke and snow,
    in secrets spoken in attentive groves.
        The voice is moving,
           feminine, bare-footed.

San Pietro prays against it.

The peacocks by the church cry out from their cage,
    calling high across the valleys.

My pen is held above the page.

It fails to connect.

*

Who says San Pietro will never relent?

A voice might have woken in a mountain cave.

I wait at the desk with wine and blank paper.

The moon is released from behind the peaks,
    tarnished by sunlight, a kernel of brass.

Mountain breezes snake down the valleys
    to freedom where the coast roads glitter
        and the Adriatic cools its sheets.

A staggering moth hits the wall, drunk on light.

The page is empty. The candle shudders.

What have I refused? How high
        could the cost have been?

Even King Tarquin saw his error.

All I can do is swallow
        the cherry stone that waiting leaves.

*

A hush descends
in the house of dusk.
The village has curled itself up.
A candle spits in the drumming silence.

Like sap leaves
a pine's trunk split
with an axe, the dead
begin to whisper. The ear. The ear.

The pen's impression
brings it through the shutters.
The ear has made it real. The dictation
of the present. The dull rally of loosened blood
sounding where the nerves ring sharp. Like footsteps
coming down a forest staircase. Is she coming? Is she? Is she?

The pines grow, the tomb is locked. San Pietro is praying against her.

The wolf will hide, the owl
will reassert its attention. The ear
is the idol of the dead. The dead cry out
but who hears them? The mists are gone in the morning.

*

Take her image, a rotted body under the roots of a pine.

We take our images as magical messages,
        the heated mind reflecting in her eyes.

What pleasures lie so locked, so hid?
　　　　Those of the image, not the ear.
　　　　　　　Take the ear as idol, source of our ailing.

San Pietro is praying. The wolf has slunk away.
The idolatry of the morbid part is deafening.
The dead speak to animals we never see.
Mists rise between the trees.

Take the ear as an image. Make her voice a picture.

The primary intention is always the image
　　　　not the ear. The owl
　　　　　　　doesn't speak. The wolf
　　　　　　　　　is a symbol.

In her oracle, sound and tongue tangle fantastically.
　　　　Few make sense of the ear's precipitations.

To know this is sickness. To hear it is wisdom. Shall we not mourn?

The ear is an idol and the dead cry out.

Her power is in the roots of a pine. So locked. And her voice?

Rising mist.

*

I was asleep before
she came. The moment
never quite happened.
The glaciers are melting.
The pines close in. The wine
turns tart and the wood
is seasoned for burning
and the fuel tank
gets empty and the hall
needs sweeping again.
From their cage by the church
the peacocks cry out.
Their cry spreads wings
and glides towards the snow tipped peaks.

Aerial

I've let it in
   through a small hole
   where the skirting-board meets the corner

I've let it in
   between the creep of waking
   and arriving tired at work

I've let it in
   on certain conditions
   and only if it keeps quiet when I say

I've let it in
   in the flash when concentration tumbles
   and the plate crashes to the floor

I've, O I've let it O
   it's in, like a cancer
   like pain trapped in its earliest memories

There's a starling on the fence and then
The wind moves and then
One hundred thousand people die in the corner of the room and then
My aerial sends its charges seeking up into the clouds and then
I inhale hard on the incense of my fetish as it floods the room and then
Everything is almost forgotten.

The word

You can repeat the same word so many times
it starts to sound strange, or foreign, and loses all meaning.

This is obvious, after the event. The glare of publicity
reproduces the word. It echoes through cable and satellite,
news report and endless analysis.

But it must also have been true before, in the quiet time
when three people gathered together in a backroom
and the word passed back and forth between them.

The event is tiny, one instance
of the word, a pinprick.

Now it goes on forever in broadcasts
rippling out across the universe
repeating and repeating

until every particle has touched it and the mind is blown apart.

Waiting for water

Fists fly out, whirling rocks: drinkers
at the bar break apart in a shower of spray.
Righting a bottle that's disgorged its froth
into an ashtray, the barmaid sighs.
I'm coming to you next Sir.

Last night I dreamed of a crab under a stone.

It's been a long dry summer.
I'm watching the flies
locked in claustrophobic loops
in the middle of the room.

I dream of a crab under a stone again and then
I can no longer drag any more dreams
from the well of sleep.

A Chinese sage, a rainmaker from Kiao-chau
visits a place where the crops are failing.
Rains return.

He needed a drink. That's why he came.
His thirst is quenched.
He leaves tomorrow.

Poker dice permutations

has the Net closed around Nothing but small fish?
do you love the world Through the eye of a Needle?
what Thoughts never admit Themselves?
did you ever make a Joke about Nostradamus?
have you let the Juice Trickle down your chin?
would this be the Ju-Ju that hinders your progress?
is Quantum theory the Noose that hangs you?
who taught the black Queen to Tango?
what Quality of light makes her eyes into Jewels?
have you been to a Quarry where Quartz is dug?
would you fast nine days in the Kingdom of the Nightingale?
did no-one explain the Kudos of the Tincture before you knocked it back?
are you anal about Keeping all your old Junk?
does Kerosene Quench your thirst?
is the Key in the way the Knot is tied?
when your nympholepsy Abates, are you Quiet?
what Jetsam has Antiquity washed you?
if you Knock on the table does Anyone knock back?
can you Apprehend the Next event?
have you been drinking sweet mint Tea with an Arab?
why are you never dealt All the Aces?

Question and answer
Jeopardy and its avoidance
how the fire is to be Kindled
at the Turn in the road
two surfaces Attracting
the Night that day makes

you keep trying to split the Air with an Axe.
no-one hails an Alabaster King.
scientists put a Kestrel in the Kiln.
the white Queen bathes alone in Absinthe.
the Knave fetches a peacock feather Quill.
no clever Quote will keep the jinn from Quitting the desert.
Albumen has filled the Jug and the yoke is lost.
the red Judge gets drunk on Kismet.
the Jackal will sing to the Quick and the dead.
when the Jaal-goat eats Juniper, only then.
Ten thousand people will still never Accept you.

you will know Them by the Knives they carry.
night will never Quell your stranger Thoughts.
the last Tiger will be killed by a Jester.
the Thief will fail because the Tide is too strong.
Nutmeg is needed to concoct the Ambrosia.
a Novocaine Kef hides the work of scribes.
you will still Question the effectiveness of Nettles.
a nomad Journeys North under sacred stars.
Trouble starts where your Nerves are sharpest.
a Nail is hammered in a Noiseless city.

Woman by a grave

The woman by the grave is not real.
This has surely been proved.
Personally, I no longer believe she existed.
I read the wrong books
and looked at the wrong paintings.
I was suffering from a kind of corruption.

Now, when I remember seeing her,
I wait until the sun comes out
and she vanishes in a non sequitur.
I say, "What woman?"
and see her grave as a Victorian cliché.

Everything about absence is real.
The real grave has no secrets.
The woman by the grave
(I never saw nor sensed her in any way)
cannot be said to have been by a real grave.
The real grave is a bright white-tiled room
somewhere else.

If the woman who stands under the birch
and stares into my upstairs window at dusk
is the woman who once stood by the grave
then it cannot be proved.

The house of the moon

Glass feathers have grown
on the window pane. The winter moon
has played the same high C all night
in coded syncopations.
Now the keyboard cover comes down
as half-light grimaces in the east.

The bedside lamp makes the room
a rosy frame around a picture
of hunched grey sky.
Glum warmth leaks from the space
where I left my crumpled sleep.

I was raised in the house of the moon.
Now I work in an office all hours of the day.
Today is the day I should refuse.
But the moon has set and my room is rented.

This is the desk, the office, the town
where capital is milked from the day.
Today is the day I should refuse.
A day I should keep for the moon.
Instead I work on columns of figures,
feeding the ashes of yesterday's fire
in someone else's house.

Unoccupied

On the washing line
a shirt hangs by its shoulders.

Open cuffs
stuck in triangular circles
pivoting on the concrete yard.

Looking at it slouch
you could never imagine it
turning up for work.

A gust of wind inflates the sleeves,
makes a kind of lifejacket.
Just for a second

everything floats...
Then a tangle of arms
destroys the metaphor.

A shirt hangs out to dry,
that's all. It's late morning.

Behaviour patterns

Butter melts in a pan,
patterned with bubbles
where the heat is underneath.
The rain last night
left trails in the sand
that read like a secret message,
a Linear B, an alien script
with uncrackable encryption.
I don't want to sleep.
I'm looking for patterns.
It's no accident.
It's what I'm programmed to do.
The stars are in constellations,
the clouds pull faces
and when breakers crash
I look for Mandelbrot patterns.
I'm a parasite feeding
on raw data.
I can't be cured.
I see patterns on patterns
of patterns until nothing
can possibly make sense.

Maps of my hermetic future

1. When we eat mandarins by the cave

2. Where we sit under a eucalyptus

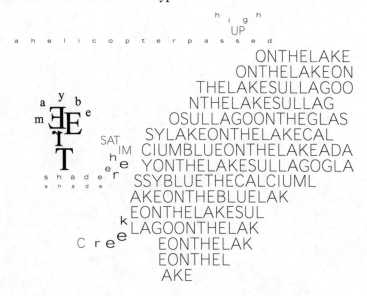

3. Climbing the narrow streets to the belltower

4. Waterfalls in the damaged valley

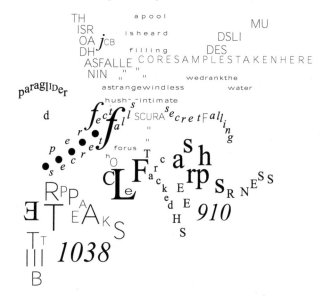

Nightwatchman

3 am. Ham sandwiches. The sentry
plays a complex but somnolent game
his blunt gentle fingertip redirecting woodlice
so they sketch him mazy networks.

A tap drips. It's like a luminous clock,
the torpid ticking cogs of his thoughts:
a fifties BSA fourstroke, chrome tank
rust freckled, petrol stagnant.

Outside the window runic bird prints
decay in a perfunctory scatter of snow.
The nightwatchman is putting on the kettle.
Now he is staring at his hands placed on his knees.

It feels like a finished New Year's Eve.
He's doing the only job he could get.
He imagines a steady drip from the sump
behind the garage door.

The window is an empty vessel,
the boiling of a Taoist kettle.
He fills his mug deliberately
as snowflakes touch the pane again.

He sips, half in a dream, gradually aware
of a child playing out in the snow.
On his feet, confused, he wets his lips
as if to speak – but the child is gone.

Words from Lara Bay

When you open your eyes underwater,
    details etched in pin-sharp air
melt into gentle waves.
    Motion blurs. Questions get hazy.
I've chosen these words
    to explain what happens
but you can't speak
    when you're not breathing.

I walk into the sea at Lara Bay.
    I walk up to my waist. Then
ducking under, I take stock
    of a world where I've always
kept my eyes closed. It's September.
    Somewhere on Lara Bay
turtle eggs are hatching,
    creatures with instincts
for a blurred world.

Six meetings in the blue book

The "Blue Book" is a journal that the author kept over several weeks prior to his death that has brought to light a mysterious young man who visited the author a number of times without explanation.

1.

I was sitting by the lake today when a young man appeared and sat down on the rock beside me.

"What's your name?" I asked.

"Nichtigall," he answered.

"*Nacht*," I mused, "and *galan*. A lover of *nachtmusik*."

"No," he said. "If my name were a riddle it would be *nichtmusik*."

I told him I thought the universe was created by the names we chose.

"Do you think so?" he said. He stood up to go.

"Do you know who I am?" I asked.

He didn't reply. I had my old leather briefcase between my feet. I lifted it up a little to give some impression of its weight.

"In here, young man," I said, "is all you need ever read about your soul."

He smiled.

"I have no soul," he said.

2.

The young man was waiting on my doorstep this morning.

"It's good of you to see me," he said, when I opened the door, "I have something for you."

He handed me a glass jar.

"What is this?" I asked.

"Volcanic ash," he said, "from Italy. Etna. You made me think of Empedocles. So here you are."

I took the jar and turned round to place it carefully on the sideboard in the hall. I inspected it for a moment in order to gather my thoughts.

"I respect your..." I said, turning back to the doorstep, but I could see the young man was already at the end of the footpath closing the garden gate.

3.

When the young man next called I took care to invite him inside without taking my eyes off him. We both sat in the leather armchairs in my study. It was just after seven in the morning. I had a visitor due at nine.

"Do you mind if I smoke?" I asked.

"Not at all," said the young man, "I'll join you."

He took a slim cigar from a fine silver case he had in the inside pocket of his jacket.

"Just a cigar," he said.

I laughed but decided to leave off my pipe until later.

"Would you care for one?" he asked.

At that point I recall the lights flickering and going out. We had been having terrible high winds. I heard the maid calling out.

"That will be the wind in the pylons," the young man said.

"'They have built the concrete that trails black wire...'" I quoted.

"So will you join me?" he asked again, holding out the silver case to me.

"Not this time, thank you," I said.

I remember the lights came back on shortly after.

4.

"I've brought you an essay," the young man said to me.

"What essay?" I asked.

"My essay," he said, "on the practice of burial."

I took it from him, cursorily scanned it and handed it back to him.

"I don't care for it," I said.

In order to explain my initial rather brusque reaction, I continued, "There are some things for which only poetry will do."

5.

"What have you for me, today?" I asked the young man as soon as he arrived. I was eager to get to the bottom of his visits.

He handed me a blank square of paper.

"Fold it once," he said.

"How?" I said.

"However you like," he said.

"Now what?"

"Fold it again."

We carried on like this until I had made six folds.

I handed the folded sheet to the young man and he opened it, smoothing it flat and examining the folds.

"So?" I said.

He produced a little notebook from the inside pocket of his jacket.

"A manual of my own devising," he said, as he started to search through the pages in the notebook.

I nodded.

"It lets me read your folds in the sheet of paper like I was reading a palm."

"So what do they say?" I asked.

He pored over the folds a while longer, counting how many times each fold was crossed by another, estimating angles. If a system is complex enough, I thought, it will yield results.

"Your reading," he said. "'You have come to believe in this reading but it's a reading that cannot be unfolded.'"

6.

I said to the young man, "Do you know who I am?"

He was silent for a long time.

In the end I asked, "What have you brought me this time?"

We were standing on the veranda and it had just started to snow. He caught a snowflake on his palm, closed his fist and proffered it.

"A kind of mandala," he said.

"Unusual," I laughed, "to have six facets."

Then, seriously, I added, "But it has no meaning, how could it be a mandala?"

"You're right," the young man said, "it's meaningless."

He opened his hand.

"It's the mandala of death."

I haven't seen the young man again.

The cycle

There's a blue moon shot with drifts of snow.
It's locked in the sky. It never moves.
The land is desolate. The night seems never ending.
I've waited eighteen hours and still the sun has not returned.
I'm going to go to sleep.

The blue moon is streaked with white discharge.
It hasn't moved.
This place is a dust bowl. Nothing grows here.
I'm feeling light, almost giddy.
I don't know what to do.

It was still night when I woke so I don't know if this was a dream
but I have just spoken with Saladin. He was crying.
I asked him, "Why are you crying?"
He said, "Because my daughter is trapped up there in the blue moon."
I looked up at it.
It hadn't moved. Curls of spume were stuck to it like lime-scale.

I won't bore you with the night's events any longer.
Suffice it to say that the sun has cut across the horizon without warning
after just under three hundred and twenty-eight hours
according to my reckoning.
This is all I can tell you
about a man's cycle.
The moon still hasn't moved.

*Note: on the moon, the earth appears stationary in the sky
and a day lasts for about a month.*

Standing

Who dreams this dream, creeping like ivy into my ear?
A man dreams it, the dreamer. He's asleep.

What does he see, this man, this dreamer who sleeps?
A young girl standing on a frozen lake, wrapped up against the cold.

This child, the lake, is that all or is there more?
The dreamer sees her kneel and wipe a gloved hand across the ice.

So the child wants to see under the ice. Can she?
The child can.

And the dreamer, can the dreamer, the man, can he see?
He sees suddenly with the eyes of the child on the frozen lake.

What is seen?
The soles of a size ten pair of hobnail boots.

She sees the bottom of some old boots?
Yes and the dreamer sees them.

And then? What does the man see then, with the child's eyes?
He sees a man in the boots, standing.

Standing?
Standing. On the other side of the ice, looking down.

Who is the man on the other side, upside down and looking through the ice?
The girl doesn't know.

Does the dreamer know, does he know the man on the other side?
No.

What happens next?
Nothing.

Analogy

The analogy came first.

When you stare straight at a dim star
it vanishes.
Then you see it
when you look away.

It was an analogy waiting to happen.

I left it waiting ten years.

Then it happened.

What I want to say
can only be said
by avoiding the subject.

Word death mandalas

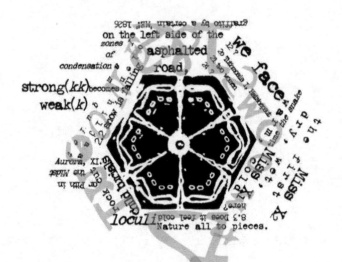

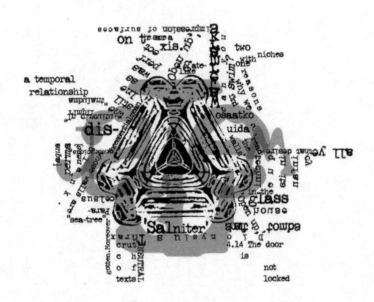

stepped

following
systematic
exposition

dromos

the

bestial body
"attains"

The duplicity

portion of Flame.

excavated

next to them

with Night

No one had tried to make a path

narcosis

Metropolis

nittäisikö se yksin täyttämään
ihmisen elämän? human shelter
modern Vandalism

After
visiting

putamina
('sharda')

necessary well

the raked paths
we take an

earth surface

there
is no

recipro

c a l

action

4.4 f

live here

PARTLY OVERGROUND

passi
ng
as I
have
the
perso
n a l
suffi
x

true reflexive

wet leather

the asphalted square

velvet
and white
cream

taloni
talosi
talonsa
talomme

the scoriae

slag

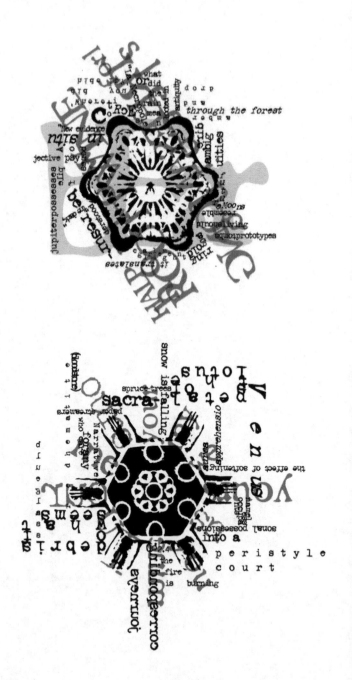

Other disguises

I might die tomorrow
and I've spent the night watching the news.
I know my time is coming.
Is it better to forget
or use every second
to think of the horror.

The evening drifts awry,
dragged by the undertow.
The inane banter we use
to fool each other
disguises a room full up
with secret worry.

Against our wills
we sit there. Like too much flour
in dough, the evening drops to bits.
We do our duty until
the conversation fails.
We die in the lulls.

There are words like eggs
stopped in my throat.
I can't speak. My days telescope.
Those wasted evenings
seem like treasures now
as I slowly get ready for bed.

Software

This is ghostless corporate daylight,
the arithmetic of flow and return.

I spin the taps, spit in the sink,
and watch the water drain away.

Each day I do unhaunted work,
shifting shadowless numbers.

It doesn't tell.
Leaves no mark.

It carries me like the flow of traffic
to the corner of a dustless room.

The ring road is never quiet.
There's a mini-bar and pay-per-view.

The sun rises and sets.
The algorithm never exits.

I look in the mirror, then look down,
lean over, and spit in the sink.

The idea of meaninglessness in Pozzuoli

Early morning, Easter Sunday. I walk
empty streets, under a sky serene, cleansed
and passionless, sea calm, sun a peach,
still unripe, while behind my sunken eyes
the hammer of black cacophony,
water and wind's plunging chaos, kept
at bay by the thought of quiet coffee,
marble bar-tops, clicking china, golden spume
and the view, empty streets, the harbour.

A haphazard church troupe emerges
from the gloom of the railway station,
dressed in white with scarlet sashes, holding
banners, pitching and lolling, and lifted behind,
the image of a cracked frescoed Madonna.
They start to play a cockeyed tarantella
on trombone, trumpet, saxophone, marching
down the early morning, almost empty street,
calling out:
   Offerta!
      Three hundred miles away
the same day begins, unseen, on a solitary hill
where wild strawberries creep around
a pile of stones I made.
   Offerta!
      Who calls up
cacophony, the procession of random events
that sticks like mud to fairy tales, and stories
painted in paradise? Overloaded meaning
turns, extreme meaning, a universe
of nothing but meaning, inverts, comes to mean
nothing, every meaning empty.

In shade by a doorway, a cat sits blinking.

I'm out of place in some random place, let's say
it might as well be Pozzuoli, three hundred
miles away, a distance designed to keep
the mind busy with difference, in giddy flight,
scanning the scene for points of reference,

in sight of the sea, salmon sky, peaches,
listing arbitrary phrases, other voices, stories
of how I get here one Easter Sunday, the grief
that's signified by wild strawberries,
the way Pozzuoli impinges, morning silk against
sleep's crumpled logic, the fresco cracked
across its cheek, plaster, dry mud, singular
uncreative sanities.

        The image of the Madonna,
propped on poles, marched along, entwines
with gaudy banners, lumpy counterpoint,
the wild hills and their secret stones,
coffee, and cracked skin, and inevitably
the blame for collisions of too much meaning:
cacophony, plunging chaos, a svelte hysteria,
the procession, the harbour, Roman remains,
the lists of valid but contingent sensations,
warm tarmac, a spilt skip, dusty cars badly parked,
a tabacchi, closed, the chance carnival
of lurching brass, the banners, pitching,
the *Offerta!*
        Che cosa?
           Soldi!
I give in. Flip an outcast's coin. What of it?
They clap their hands, dispelling the pain of loss.
The future shoots skyward like a rocket
then breaks in a shower of green sparks.
A serenely bitter man stands meaninglessly
in the shade of a lime tree. The perfume
is a flood of paisley that can't be allowed
to have meaning. Not here and now. Not
today. I entwine my fingers in the leaves,
ask the Madonna if it'll be over soon,
or is it over already, has it turned?
Laboured insight and careful observation
haven't extracted a pip from the event.
Mud sticks, the fresco dries, the metaphors
collide, meaning hopelessness, cleansed
bitter grief and a pile of stones
where wild strawberries grow on the hillside.

The carnival has gone

Half six and I'm barefoot in the kitchen
waiting for the kettle. The steam is massing.
Through unbright eyes I focus thoughtlessly
until my dreams hush like an audience and I remember
the carnival has gone.

I'm making notes on a carnival that exists only as it leaves.

I can hear rain on a patch of dried grass.
I want to be in bed pretending to sleep
so I can lie awake secretly and listen
to the last shreds of night music. But it's morning now,
the carnival has gone.

That patch of dried grass
        could be the result of any number of phenomena.

I'm trained up like a monkey.
When the music stops the conditioned reflex
drops like a curtain. The wrong spell
blinds intention. The stage is empty,
the carnival gone.

There's really no point going on about it any more.

Other books published by Oversteps

Anthologies: Company of Poets and Company of Four
David Grubb: An Alphabet of Light
Giles Goodland: Littoral
Alex Smith: Keyserling
Will Daunt: Running out of England
Patricia Bishop: Saving Dragons & Time's Doppelgänger
Christopher Cook: For and Against Nature
Jan Farquarson: No dammed tears
Charles Hadfield: The nothing we sink or swim in
Mandy Pannett: Bee Purple & Frost Hollow
Doris Hulme: Planted with stones
James Cole: From the Blue
Helen Kitson: Tesserae
Bill Headdon: Picardy.com
Avril Bruten: In the lost & found columns
Ross Cogan: Stalin's desk
Ann Kelley: Because we have reached that place
Marianne Larsen: A Common Language
Anne Lewis-Smith: Every seventh wave
Mary Maher: green darlings
Susan Taylor: The suspension of the moon
Simon Williams: Quirks
Genista Lewis: Cat's Cradle
Alwyn Marriage: Touching Earth
Miriam Darlington: Windfall
Anne Born & Glen Phillips: Singing Granites
A C Clarke: Messages of Change
Rebecca Gethin: River is the Plural of Rain
W H Petty: But someone liked them
Melanie Penycate: Feeding Humming Birds

www.overstepsbooks.com